100 Irish Sayings, Toasts and Blessings

Revised Edition

By James O'Shea
(c) *2014*

The Illustrations for this book were found in the following source periodicals circa

1845-1852:
The Illustrated London News
The Pictorial Times
and
The Oxford to Skibbereen

Dedicated to my lovely mother Eileen Marie and my dear sweet aunt Bonnie.

100 Irish Sayings, Toasts and Blessings

Preface: The following are not all poems, therefore they will not always rhyme. They are a collection of various Irish sayings, toasts, and blessings that have either been commonly used in colloquial Irish speech throughout the last century, or are quite archaic and have been retooled slightly to be more agreeable to the modern ear, or else in some cases, have been passed down verbally through the generations of my own family. All that said, I hope you will all enjoy them as much as my dear sweet mother and aunt did.

James O'Shea

11

100 Irish Sayings

God needed laughter in the world,
So He made the Irish race.
For they always meet life with a smile,
And rosy cheeks upon their face.

There's Music in the names of the Irish,
And Magic in their laughter.
May it bring you Good Luck,
Here and ever after.

Grant us a sense of humor, O'Lord,
The saving grace to laugh, and smile, and to tell a joke.
To win some happiness out of this life,
And then pass it on to other folk.

May the lilt of Irish laughter
Lighten every load.
And may you taste a bit of life's simple pleasures,
Those that fortune chose to bestow.

May you live to be 100...
Plus an extra year to Repent!

14

An Irish blessing
From the heart of a true friend,
May good fortune forever be
yours,
And may your joys never end.

May your Irish heart always
be light and merry,
And your cares few.
May your troubles all vanish,
And may your wishes
All come true.

Ireland, with her enchanted
hills of emerald green,
To stroll her shamrock covered
sod
Is to touch a bit of Heaven,
And walk hand in hand with
God.

May those that love us, love us.
And those that don't,
May The Good Lord God turn
their hearts.
And if He doesn't turn their
hearts,
May He turn their ankles,
So that we'll know them by
their limp.

Oh, for fuck's sake.

May you be blessed with the strength of Heaven
The light of the Sun and the radiance of the Moon
The splendor of fire
The speed of lightning
The swiftness of wind
The depth of the sea
The stability of the Earth
And the firmness of rock.

[From the 4th Century armor breastplate of our own beloved Saint Patrick]

Here's to Erin!
The land of the brave and the bold.

May we have those in our arms
That we truly love deep in our hearts.

Here's to you and yours,
And to mine and ours,
And if mine and ours ever come
Across you and yours,
I hope you and yours will do
As much for mine and ours,
As mine and ours have done
For you and yours!

May the Lord keep you
In the hollow of His hand,
And never close His fist too tight!

Grand. Simply grand.

May you be in Heaven a half
hour
Before the Devil knows you're
dead.
(older version)

May you have food and
raiment *(clothing)*
And a soft pillow for your head.
May you be forty years in
Heaven
Before the Devil knows you're
dead.

The first hundred years are always the hardest...
It gets easier after that.

If that's the worst thing that ever happens to you,
You'll be alright.

May the cadence of an Irish jig
Wash your cares away,
And the warmth of Irish laughter
Fill all your days.

Here's to:
The health of our sweethearts, and our wives...
May they never meet.

As we all toil amongst the
fray, and occasionally lose our
way,
May Irish angels walk along
beside you,
Each and every day.

Here's to:
The land of the Shamrock
Where Irish hearts run true.
Here's to our blessed patron
Saint Patrick.
But most of all, my friend,
here's to you.

Here's to:
A bit of Ale
And a bit of cheer,
And a guardian angel
Always near.

Here's to Ireland:
The fairest place on earth,
That Heaven herself has doth
kissed,
With gentle melodies, and mirth,
And meadows filled with clover
and mist.

May green grass grow long
and lush
On that sad and dreary road to
Hell,
From so many years of neglect
and want of use.

May the roof above us never
fall in!
And may we friends gathered
here,
In the house below it,
Never fall out.

Here's to:
A bit of Irish luck,
Music and cheer,
Good friends and laughter,
Each and every day of the
year.

Here's to a woman's kiss,
And to whiskey, amber clear;
Not as sweet as a woman's kiss,
But a damn sight more sincere!

Here's to the love that lies
deep inside every woman's soft
and tender eyes,
And lies, and lies, and lies.

Fair young maidens want
nothing more than husbands,
And when they have them, then
they want everything else.

Here's to Women:
The source of all men's bliss,
A simple taste of Heaven hidden
in each tender but fleeting kiss.
But from the Queen in England,
To the wench working the dairy
They all have one thing in
common,
They're all really quite
contrary.

Here's to:
The health of all the pretty
young lasses!

Here's to the lass I truly love
And here's to the lass that loves
me,
And here's to all the other
lasses I haven't met yet.

There is nothing stronger
than Love,
Nothing higher, wider, deeper,
Nothing more bitter sweet,
Nothing more cherished,
Nothing more desired or
misunderstood,
And nothing more pleasant.

Here's to:
The prettiest
The wittiest
The truest of all those who are
true,
But most of all, my beloved,
Here's to you.

Here's to Forgotten Loves:
If Discord had never thrown
her cursed apple,
Then poor old Paris would
never have had to choose,
Between the loveliest Goddesses
in Heaven,
Knowing that two of them
would have to lose.

May we all be lucky enough to
be blessed with the unfleeting
love of one, the friendship of
many, and the good will of all.

Here's to why God made
alcohol:
So that the Irish wouldn't rule
the world.

Here's to a temperance
supper,
With water in glasses clear and
tall,
And coffee and tea to end with,
And me not there at all.

Here's to:
A long life, and a merry one.
A quick death, and a painless one.
A pretty girl, and an honest one.
A frosty pint--- and another
one!

When life is at it's gloomiest,
and all seems dreary,
Remember this, my little lass,
That life looks much rosier
Through the bottom of a glass.

May we all die a happy death,
To merrily drown drinking
with Bacchus,
Rather than dying for Mars.

May Joy and Happiness always
be your companions
On the road of life,
And may you always manage to
avoid those trouble makers,
Discord and Strife.

May you be poor in
Misfortune,
Rich in Blessings
Slow to make enemies
Quick to make friends
But rich or poor,
Quick or slow,
May you know nothing but
Happiness
Each and every day
From this day forward.

May Good Fortune follow you
all of your days,
And Trouble never catch up.

Ireland, the land of the Great
Gaels
The men that God doth made
mad
For all their Wars were merry
And all their songs are sad.

May God with his infinite
compassion
Look over you, here and ever
after,
And may the Devil always be in
want of spectacles.

May the hinges of our
Friendship never rust.

Here's to:
Precious old Ireland,
The lovely emerald isle.
To her Irish laughter,
And her Irish whiskey,
And to every pretty colleens
smile,
To her lullabies, and her Irish
jigs,
To her rolling hills of shamrock
and clover,
To her mist and her music,
And to the leprechauns too.
But most of all my friends,
Here's to all of you.

Here's to:
The land of the shamrock, so
green, and oh so dear,
To each Irish lad, and his pretty
and beloved colleen.
Here's to the ones we love
dearest and most.
And may God save our blessed
Old Ireland!
That's an Irishman's toast.

A simple Irish toast
From the county of Kerry,
To you and all of yours,
May all your days be sunny,
And all your nights merry!

May Good Fortune be yours
And may your joys never end.

To all my friends, far and
near,
To all those gathered here,
May you all find Love, and
happiness,
And may the soft lilt of Irish
laughter
Forever tickle your ear.

The Irish are a cheerful lot,
big hearted and true,
For they laugh and sing, and
never grow weary...
Of adding a little bit of color to
life's somber hue,
Making this world just a little
less dreary.

May your blessings be many
And your troubles few.

Bless your little Irish heart,
And all the rest of you too.

Here's to Women:
The better half of man.

May the Good Saints look over
and protect us all our days.
But may they lose sight of us
here this night,
In the midst of this Pub's smoky
haze. Amen.

The Rose and the Shamrock
Will always remind me,
Of the quiet lanes and hills
That I left far behind me.

Sweet Mother Ireland
The Fairest of all the lands.
The mist upon Her meadows
Lay close to every Irish heart.

May the Good Saint Patrick
give you a happy heart,
And keep you well throughout
the year.

May we be rich in friends
rather than gold.

May our beloved Saint Patrick,
forever walk by your side.
And when you're done with this
life,
May the Good Saint Peter
Open the pearly gates of
Heaven extra wide.

May our beloved Saint Patrick,
Whom we all so dearly cherish
and adore,
Intercede before the presence
of evil and misfortune,
And bring you nothing but
blessings from above, and good
fortune laid at your door.

May the Good Saint Patrick
shield and protect us
From the snares of the heathen
Devils
Who wish to do us ill,
Alone or in multitude.

May Good Luck find you,
And the Good Fates grant you,
All that your hearts be wishing,
To you and all of yours,
From this day forward and
forever more,
Until you attain all your
desires and ambitions.

May the face of all good news
And the backside of all bad,
Be facing toward us, now and
All our days.

Long live the Irish!
Long live their cheer!
Long live this blessed marriage
Year After Year!

May the sound of joyful music
And the soft lilt of Irish
laughter,
Forever fill your days,
Here and forever after.

God bless you, now and always
With the gift of Irish cheer.

Near the misty streams and babbling brooks
Of the rolling green hills of our beloved Mother Ireland,
Inside the hollows of old knotted oak trees,
Live mystical, mythical, magical leprechauns,
Who are clever as can be.

With pointed ears and turned up noses
And little wool coats of green,
They bowl all day, drinking beer,
While trying hard not to be seen.

Only those of us who truly believe,
Can see these little bearded men dressed in green,
But be mindful when you do, my friends,
Because they're a tricky lot,
And honestly, they're really quite mean.

In the coming New Year,
May your right hand always
Be stretched out in Friendship
And never in want.

May the blessings of the Irish
be many,
Where ever your path may
wind,
May every day that's coming,
Be better than the one you left
behind.

May you always receive a kindly greeting,
From all those you meet upon the road.

Top of the morning!

May the road rise to meet you,
May the wind be always at your back,
The sunshine warm upon your face,
The rain fall soft upon your fields,
And, until we meet again,
May The Lord God hold you in the hollow of His hand.

70

May you have warm words on
a cold evening,
A full moon on a dark and
cloudy night,
The road covered with
shamrocks,
And eternally tilted downhill.

May the Good Saint Patrick
Always keep you in his care,
May the luck of the Irish
always be with you,
And your seas always be fair.

72

May the Luck of the Irish be
with you, where ever you go,
And may the Good Blessings of
our dear Saint Patrick
outnumber the bad ones,
And all the emerald shamrocks
that grow.

Wherever you go and
whatever you do,
May the luck of the Irish
always be there with you.

It would take more lucky
shamrocks
Than Ireland ever grew,
To bring the luck and good
fortune,
That I'm wishing upon you.

May the sweet cadence of
quiet Gaelic lullabies,
And the gentle giggles of a
child's laughter,
Forever fill these days,
Here and forever after.

As the Good Saint Patrick
used to say,
If you're lucky enough to be
Irish,
Then you're lucky enough.

May the Patron Saint of
Ireland
The Good Saint Patrick himself,
Opus Dei,
Bless you with the luck of the
Irish
Each and every day.

Sure I is and sure I'll be
That what I say is true,
That the luck of the Irish was
with me,
On the day that I met you.

78

'Tis glad I am
And glad I'll be
Knowin' you likes
The likes of me.

The Irish are the luckiest folk
in the world,
Or so I've been told,
Because at the end of every
Irish rainbow,
Lies a shining pot of gold.

May your troubles be less
And your blessings be more
And no one else but Lady Luck
Come a walking through that
door.

And that's no blarney.

An Exile's toast:

Remember where ever our
goblet is crowned,
Throughout this world, and into
the next,
Whether eastward or
westward we roam,
When the smile of a dear
woman goes round,
Oh! Remember the smile which
adorns her, your true Love,
Back at home.

Here's to both Ireland and
America together:
May the former soon be as
free as the latter,
And may the latter never
forget that it was the Irishman
Who was instrumental in
securing that liberty that they
now so easily enjoy.

The Irish pray on their knees,
While the English prey on
their neighbors.

If we do not succeed, glorious
Old Ireland, to set you free,
May the English hang us high
from the nearest gooseberry
tree.

Here's to Liberty all over the world,
And everywhere else too.

Oh, I'd be an awful fool
If I didn't know that.

May the Good Lord take a liking to you, ...
But not too soon!

Like the Virgin Mary once said,
Come again?

Erin go braugh!

(Gaelic for "Ireland Forever!")

Made in the USA
Las Vegas, NV
17 January 2023

65793331R00059